C000125246

Making the most of your child's baptism

A gift for all the family

Ally Barrett

For churches: A supporting leaflet for churches with tips on using this book in baptism preparation and further good-practice ideas is available to download from www.spckpublishing.co.uk.

First published in Great Britain in 2011

Society for Promoting Christian Knowledge
36 Causton Street
London SW1P 4ST
www.spckpublishing.co.uk

British Library Cataloguing-in-Publication Data
A catalogue record for this book is available from the British Library

ISBN 978–0–281–06461–8

1 3 5 7 9 10 8 6 4 2

Designed and typeset by Sarah Smith
Interior images: © Shutterstock Images. Pages 8 and 18 © Rene Schulz
and page 12 by Sarah Smith.
Printed in China by New Era

About this book

You're probably reading this book because you would like your child to be baptized, which is a wonderful thing to do.

Baptism is a very special event in your child's life. It's your child's first step on a journey of faith.

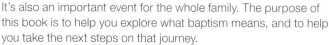

It's also an important event for the whole family. The purpose of this book is to help you explore what baptism means, and to help you take the next steps on that journey.

Making the Most of Your Child's Baptism aims to:
- explain what baptism is and explore the baptism service;
- suggest ways of helping your child grow up as part of God's family;
- suggest ways in which your child's baptism can help the whole family grow in faith together.

We hope you'll enjoy and treasure this book for many years to come.

A note about words
You might be more familiar with the term 'christening' than 'baptism'. The two words mean the same thing, but we've used the word 'baptism' throughout.

This book includes some words from the baptism service. There is more than one version of the service. The version given here is used in most churches. If your church uses slightly different wording, the person who takes you through the service will explain the differences to you.

A note on icons
The following icons are used in this book:

  Words from the baptism service itself

  An explanation of the words of the text

  Questions for you to consider

  An idea or activity to try at home

Why bring your child for baptism?

There might be many reasons why you'd like your child to be baptized. Here are a few that parents give.

- 'The gift of a child is like a miracle. We and our wider family want to come to church to say thank you for this incredible gift.'
- 'Having children baptized or christened is a tradition in our family.'
- 'Having a faith is important to us and we'd like our child to share it.'
- 'We believe it's the "proper" thing to do.'
- 'Baptizing our child means that we'll all become part of "something bigger".'

The arrival of a child often makes people look at life differently. Perhaps such a major change in your life has made you think about your own faith. So now might be a good time to explore the Christian faith and think about your own commitment to God.

Even if you've been a Christian for a long time, becoming a parent or godparent can still be a chance to get to know God in a new way, and to take a big step forward on your journey of faith.

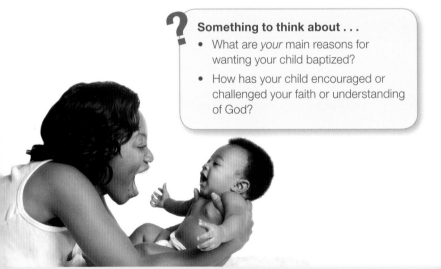

? Something to think about . . .
- What are *your* main reasons for wanting your child baptized?
- How has your child encouraged or challenged your faith or understanding of God?

Baptism: the start of a journey

Baptism is an opportunity to thank God for the gift of a child.

But it also means that your child becomes a member of God's family, the Church, and sets out to live as a child of God. Baptism is the first step on a journey of faith, a journey that will take a lifetime.

Baptism is one of what the church calls 'sacraments'. Sacraments use symbols to show that something real is happening spiritually, even though it can't be seen. The symbols of baptism – water, the sign of the cross and a lighted candle – focus on new life, belonging to God and what it means to live in the world as a Christian.

Jesus himself was baptized as an adult. One of the readings often used in the baptism service describes this event.

Mark 1.9–11
Jesus came from Nazareth in Galilee, and John baptized him in the River Jordan. As soon as Jesus came out of the water, he saw the sky open and the Holy Spirit coming down to him like a dove. A voice from heaven said,
'You are my own dear Son, and I am pleased with you.'

God spoke these wonderful words before Jesus had done any miracles or told any parables. These words weren't a reward for the good things that Jesus had done, but a starting point for all that he would go on to do in his life and ministry.

How might it feel to add your own name at the beginning of those words of God, and hear him say to you:
'. . . . . , **you are my child, I love you, and I am pleased with you'**? Being loved by God isn't a reward for everything we've done right, but a starting point for all that we'll do in our lives.

Baptism: joining the Church

Baptisms may take place during a normal Sunday church service or at some other time. Whenever the baptism happens, the Church will be happy to take the opportunity to welcome your child into God's family.

Christians come in all shapes and sizes – most churches have a mixture of men and women, and younger and older people; all will be at different stages on their journeys of faith. Churches today try to be places where everyone can grow to know God better and support one another.

There are more tips about becoming part of the church family on page 19.

Your local church is part of God's worldwide family. When we join the Church, we become part of a community that's been growing for 2,000 years and has members in every nation on earth!

? **Something to think about . . .**
Think about the people, organizations, communities and networks that support you. What support would you value from your local church at this stage of your life?

What about godparents?

Parents and godparents have a very important part to play in baptism. New parents often need all the help they can get, and this applies to the Christian life too. As your child grows, he or she will need supporters on the journey of faith.

It's usual to have three godparents, two of the same sex as your child and one of the opposite sex.

What makes a good godparent?

- A godparent is someone who will accompany your child on the journey of faith. This journey is an ongoing one that we all share. Every one of us is a 'work in progress', so nobody expects godparents to have all the answers about life, the universe and everything! But it will be good for your child to have godparents to turn to whenever he or she needs them.

- Because baptism is the start of a journey of faith, it's important that godparents are on a similar journey, so they can help your child to develop in faith and come to know God. For this reason, godparents themselves have to have been baptized – it's a sign that they are also on a journey of faith.

? **Something to think about . . .**
What do you hope for in your child's godparents
- on the day of baptism?
- in a year's time?
- in ten years' time?
- in thirty years' time?

The baptism service

On the next few pages, we'll take you step by step through the baptism service.

In baptism, the Church is delighted to welcome your child as a new member. God's people have a responsibility to welcome, nurture and encourage the newly baptized child. So, at the start of the baptism part of the service, the minister asks a question of the 'people of God':

> Faith is the gift of God to his people.
> In baptism the Lord is adding to our number those whom he is calling.
> People of God, will you welcome
> *this child* and uphold *him/her*
> in *his/her* new life in Christ?
> **With the help of God, we will.**

With this encouragement and the welcome of the church family, you (parents and godparents) can feel supported in the promises you're about to make.

The priest asks you the following questions about helping the child to grow in faith.

> Will you pray for *him/her*,
> draw *him/her* by your example
> into the community of faith
> and walk with *him/her*
> in the way of Christ?
> **With the help of God, we will.**

Something to think about . . .
- Leading by example happens whether we want it to or not! Which of your own habits and characteristics would you want your child to learn from you?
  Are there any you'd rather your child didn't pick up?
- Think about your own understanding of God: what would you like your child to learn about who God is and why faith matters?

In baptism this child begins *his/her* journey in faith.
You speak for *him/her* today.
Will you care for *him/her*,
and help *him/her* to take *his/her* place
within the life and worship of Christ's Church?
With the help of God, we will.

How can you and your local church make sure that your child feels at home in church and at home with God?

What can adults learn about God and faith from children?

In what practical ways can you take part in the life and worship of your local church?

Something to think about . . .
How will each of you (parents and godparents) care for your child as he or she develops mentally, emotionally and spiritually?

9

The decision

The decision

In baptism, God calls us out of darkness
into his marvellous light.
To follow Christ means dying to sin
and rising to new life with him.
Therefore I ask:

Do you turn to Christ?
I turn to Christ.

Do you repent of your sins?
I repent of my sins.

Do you renounce evil?
I renounce evil.

A candle is lit as a symbol of the light of God. Here, we turn away from all that is dark and turn towards Jesus Christ, the source of all that is light and good.

As you say these words, why not silently 'name and shame' the darkness in the world around you and in your own life? Ask God to shine his light into your heart.

We sometimes talk about the light of truth or hope or love. People may light candles to remember loved ones who have died. Light a candle and look at the flame and feel its warmth. What does it make you think or feel?

 Sit down and watch the news one evening. For each item, light a small candle (such as a tea light) and ask for God's blessing to be in that situation. If the news is bad, pray for those who seem to be suffering most, and also for those who seem to be responsible.

 Find a map of your local area and trace each street or location with your finger, or even go for a walk round your neighbourhood. As you do so, think about where the darkness is in those places – perhaps it's in divisions between different communities or a spot where you know people are suffering.

 Something to think about . . .
- Who is bringing light into those situations?
- How can you and your family be involved in bringing God's light into a world that sometimes seems too dark?

The signing with the cross

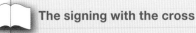

The signing with the cross

The priest makes the sign of the cross on the child's forehead:

[*Child's name*], Christ claims you for his own.
Receive the sign of his cross.
Do not be ashamed to confess
the faith of Christ crucified.
**Fight valiantly as a disciple of Christ
against sin, the world and the devil,
and remain faithful to Christ
to the end of your life.**

May almighty God deliver you
from the powers of darkness,
restore in you the image of his glory,
and lead you in the light
and obedience of Christ.
Amen.

The cross is the sign of Jesus Christ. It shows that your child belongs not only to himself or herself, nor just to you, but also to God.

We don't set out to be 'against' the world, as if the world were always a bad place (though so often it isn't how God wants it to be); but when it seems that the world is against us, we need to stand firm and hold on to what we believe, knowing that we aren't alone.

The cross is the sign of Jesus Christ.

Jesus died on a cross to show the world how much God loves us and that there's nothing he wouldn't do to save us.

No one can see the sign of the cross that's made in a baptism service. Even if oil or water is used, it quickly fades.

But your child will know that the cross is there because, when he or she is older, you'll be able to tell him or her about it, and hopefully your child will live life in a way that shows he or she belongs to God.

We all face choices every day:

- at work
- at home
- with friends or neighbours
- in the way we spend our money
- in the way we spend our time.

When you're next faced with a challenge that you think might be too much for you or you just feel the world is against you, take a few seconds to trace the sign of the cross on your forehead. As you do, simply ask God to help you make the right choices, and to help you live the way you want to live and the way you know you should live.

The prayer over the water

The prayer over the water

Some of the following words and ideas might be included in the prayer:

We thank you, almighty God for the gift of water to sustain, refresh and cleanse all life.

Over water, the Holy Spirit moved in the beginning of creation.

Through water you led the children of Israel from slavery in Egypt to freedom in the Promised Land.

Water is vital for the body and God's Holy Spirit is vital for spiritual life. We pray that God will use this water as a way for us to receive the new life he wants to give.

At creation, God made order out of chaos. His presence can do the same in our lives.

God held back the water of the Red Sea so that his people could escape. His grace also enables us to be set free from the things that stop us living our lives fully.

In baptism, God washes away all the things about us that aren't life-giving. We are 'born again' to have a fresh start and live our lives as children of God. When Jesus died and came alive again, he showed us that the life and love of God are stronger than death. At baptism, we receive that life and love of God.

We thank you, Father,
for the water of baptism.
In it we are buried
with Christ in his death.
By it we share in his resurrection.
Through it we are reborn
by the Holy Spirit . . .

Now sanctify this water . . .

Renewed in your image,
may they walk by the light of faith . . .

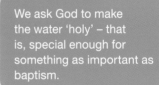

We ask God to make the water 'holy' – that is, special enough for something as important as baptism.

What kind of God do we believe in?

We affirm our faith

Do you believe and trust in God the Father,
source of all being and life,
the one for whom we exist?
I believe and trust in him.

Do you believe and trust in God the Son,
who took our human nature,
died for us and rose again?
I believe and trust in him.

Whenever we pray 'Our Father . . .', it reminds us that God made us and never stops loving us.

The love we feel for our own children is only a shadow of how much God loves us.

We believe that Jesus is God's Son and that he came to live as one of us. By knowing Jesus, we can know God. Jesus embraced outcasts and people whom nobody else valued. He showed us a better way to live. He ultimately died to demonstrate how much God loves us, and came alive again to show that the love of God is stronger than death.

? **Something to think about . . .**
If Jesus were to come to earth today, where would he go and who would he spend his time with?

Do you believe and trust in God the Holy Spirit, who gives life to the people of God and makes Christ known in the world?
I believe and trust in him.

The Holy Spirit is God's way of being with us – in every place and at every time – and with each person. When children are baptized, we pray especially that God's Holy Spirit will be with them so they know that God is with them every day of their lives.

Something to think about . . .
Have there been times when you've been especially aware that God is with you – perhaps during a major crisis, at a time of decision-making or at a moment of real inner peace?

This is the faith of the Church.
This is our faith.
We believe and trust in one God:
Father, Son and Holy Spirit.
Amen.

Your child is baptized in the name of God: Father, Son and Holy Spirit. This faith is one we share with all God's people throughout the world.

The baptism

The baptism

The minister pours water on the child, saying

[*Child's name*], I baptize you
in the name of the Father,
and of the Son,
and of the Holy Spirit.
Amen.

What's in a name?
Names are important. You probably spent a long time choosing your child's name. You might also have looked up the origin of the name and what it means.

Baptism isn't a naming ceremony. But using your child's full name in church during the baptism service is a powerful way of admitting that he or she belongs not just to you, but to God.

God says: 'Do not be afraid, for I have redeemed you, I have called you by your name, you are mine' (Isaiah 43.1).

The welcome

There is one Lord, one faith, one baptism:
[*Child's name*], by one Spirit we are all baptized into one body.
**We welcome you into the fellowship of faith;
we are children of the same heavenly Father;
we welcome you.**

Being baptized is about deepening our relationship with God and his people.

Becoming part of the church family

- If the baptism is taking place during a main church service, you'll meet some of the church family (if you haven't already done so). If the baptism is taking place in a separate service, find out when the regular services are, so that you can get to know some of the other members of God's family in your local area.

- Find out what your local church has on offer for children and families. Which services are most child-friendly? Is there a network or newsletter, a mums-and-tots group, or special events for children and families? If there aren't any yet, you could encourage the church to start something and get involved yourself, beginning with other families who have recently had a child baptized.

- Don't forget to keep in touch with your church after the baptism – tell them if you move house. Don't be afraid to ask for their help if you're in difficulty – even if there's nothing else they can do, they'll always be happy to pray for you.

Prayers

The Prayers
A minister prays for your child, for you and the godparents, and may also mention issues in the world and those in need. The prayers may end with this version of the Lord's Prayer or a modern one.

**Our Father, who art in heaven,
hallowed be thy name.
Thy kingdom come, thy will be done
on earth as it is in heaven.
Give us this day our daily bread.
And forgive us our trespasses,
as we forgive those who trespass against us.
And lead us not into temptation;
but deliver us from evil.
For thine is the kingdom, the power and the glory,
for ever and ever. Amen.**

Jesus taught his friends what we now know as the Lord's Prayer. In it, Jesus shows us how to:

- pray that the world might increasingly become the place God created it to be ('Thy kingdom come . . .');

- ask for the basic things we need and for help to ensure that others' needs are also met ('Give us this day . . .');

- admit that we often need God's help to stop holding grudges and to give one another (and ourselves) a second (third or fourth . . .) chance ('And forgive us our trespasses . . .');

- ask God to help us stay strong when we face tough decisions in life or face danger, as well as living out our day-to-day responsibilities ('deliver us from evil . . . ').

Giving of the lighted candle

Giving of the lighted candle
Your child is given a candle which may be lit from the Easter Candle.

God has delivered us from the dominion of darkness and has given us a place with the saints in light.

You have received the light of Christ;
walk in this light all the days of your life.
**Shine as a light in the world
to the glory of God the Father.**

Our prayer for newly baptized children is that they will shine with the light of God every day of their lives, and so make the world around them a brighter, better place. This commission is one that we can all accept and try to live out, with God's help.

Try singing this song to your child:

This little light of mine, I'm gonna let it shine.
This little light of mine, I'm gonna let it shine.
This little light of mine, I'm gonna let it shine.
Let it shine, let it shine, let it shine.

Keep your child's baptism candle in a safe place (or even have it on display). Light it on each anniversary of the baptism to remind your child that the light of God shines in him or her.

After baptism: what next?

You'll have made some big promises about the way you'll help your child to grow in faith. What do those promises look like in real life? The next few pages give you some ideas.

'Will you pray for them?'

What is prayer?
Prayer is a conversation with God.

Sometimes it's good to talk to God using a traditional prayer, such as the Lord's Prayer (see page 20), but sometimes it's good to pray in your own words. If you can't find any words, you can still bring to God all that's on your mind and heart.

God will always hear us, even if we've never spoken to him before, but it's good to get into the habit of praying regularly – not just in a crisis.

A conversation is a two-way process. We can spend time quietly in God's presence, listening and waiting for new ideas to come into our minds about our daily lives – people to help, relationships to mend and wrongs to put right.

Just as conversations with other people help us to get to know them, so conversation with God helps us to grow closer to him.

Do I have to be quiet?

It might help to go somewhere you're able to have time to yourself. Setting aside time can be hard when you have a young family, so don't worry if you can't find more than a very short time to pray or if you have to pray while you're doing something else (commuting, ironing, gardening or even taking a shower). You can pray anywhere and at any time – when you're walking, standing, sitting or doing whatever feels comfortable.

Closing your eyes might help you to avoid distractions, but sometimes the distractions can become part of your prayers. For instance, if there's a lot of traffic noise, you might pray for the safety of those travelling; or if your baby wakes up just when you're trying to pray, use that as an opportunity to ask God to bless him or her.

Praying for your child

You've promised to pray for your child. What sort of things will you pray about? Spend some time thinking about your hopes, fears and dreams for your child. Be as honest as you can.

When I pray for [*Name*] . . . .

I am thankful for . . . .

I worry about . . . .

I hope for . . . .

Praying for yourself

Now try thinking about yourself. What are you thankful for in your own life? What are the things you worry about for yourself? What are your own hopes and dreams for the future?

Praying for the world

Now try thinking about the world. What things in the world around you make you want to say thank you (a beautiful sunset, a good news story . . .)? What issues in the world are you afraid of or angry about (economic crisis, climate change, injustice . . .)? What, in your heart of hearts, do you wish for the world (peace, an end to suffering . . .)?

Sometimes it helps to have some set words for prayer. Here are some that might be helpful.

A prayer for parents and godparents
(based on the three main symbols used in baptism)

Lord Jesus, may the sign of your cross
keep me strong and faithful when life is hard.

When I am tired or burdened
by things I have done wrong,
refresh me and wash me clean.

The world sometimes seems a very dark place.
Shine your light in my heart
and help me to shine as a light for others.
Amen.

Heavenly Father, bless all those I love
and all those I find it hard to love.
Amen.

God of love, even in times of anger,
help me not to fight evil with evil.
May I never let the sun go down on my anger,
but always look for reconciliation,
understanding, peace, or – if all else fails –
an ending everyone can live with.
Amen.

Breton fisherman's prayer
Dear God, be good to me;
the sea is so wide, and my boat is so small.
Amen.

Praying with your child

It's never too early to start praying *with* children, as well as *for* them. Even very young children can enjoy and benefit from a regular 'night-night' prayer as part of the bedtime routine. Some simple ideas are given here.

- 'God bless . . .' adding the names of friends, family, etc. Often toddlers will start to suggest names to add.
- 'Thank you for . . .' mentioning favourite things that have happened during the past day.

  You can use this time as an opportunity to talk to your child about what has happened during the day.

- Praying for a friend or family member who's in particular need (such as a serious illness).

  Praying with your child for that person can be a good way of explaining the situation and acknowledging your own feelings about it.

Older children might like to learn 'finger prayers' that help them remember what to include in their own prayers. One traditional version suggests:

- **the thumb**: make a 'thumbs-up' sign and say thank you for good things that have happened;
- **the index ('pointing') finger**: point into the distance and ask God for guidance about a decision or difficult situation;
- **the middle (biggest) finger**: pray for people who are'strong' or powerful in the world (such as the Prime Minister and the government, and the leaders of other countries) or in the child's own life (such as teachers);
- **the ring finger**: pray for people we love – family and friends;
- **the little finger**: pray for people who are 'weak' or 'small' in the eyes of the world – those who get overlooked or who are in trouble.

Not just words...

Children are often especially responsive to prayers that use several of their senses. There are lots of ways to encourage your child to grow spiritually. Here are some ideas that parents have tried and recommended.

- Many children enjoy hugging a very soft cushion as a way of expressing love for God or enjoying God's love for them, or expressing concern for people they know are in need.

- Make a pompom out of blue and green wool (so that it looks a little like a globe). Think about how it feels to work hard to make something special, and how protective we feel about it when we've made it. While your child holds the pompom carefully, talk about God creating the world and loving it – you could read the story of creation together from a children's Bible.

- Let your child rub child-friendly skin cream into your hand, as you also rub it into his or hers. As you do so, think about the people you know who need special care, attention and love.

- Light a candle and spend some time quietly looking at the flame and enjoying its warmth and light. Think of people who are struggling and who would love to feel that kind of warmth and light in their lives. (NB: always keep candles out of the reach of children when you're not there; never leave a lit candle unattended.)

- Find a very fluffy feather and take turns to blow on it gently. Or, on a windy day, watch the movement of the treetops. Enjoy the mystery of all the things that we can't see (like air, like love, like God) but know are real because we can see the effect they have on us and on the world.

- Set aside a corner somewhere in the house where you can put 'holy' things, which might include a children's Bible, a cross or a candle (but not the matches). You could also include special objects that your child has enjoyed collecting, such as pebbles, feathers and any bits and bobs that you've used in your 'sensory' prayers, as well as photographs of family members who are far away.

- Allow yourself time to share your child's wonder at the world. Every so often, leave plenty of time to walk, to stop and look at things: a spider's web covered with dew; the skeleton of a leaf, an interesting pebble, a hole in the road, the shapes in the clouds, the reflections in a muddy puddle . . .

Songs

This is the way we pray to God,
pray to God, pray to God.
This is the way we pray to God,
we know that he will hear us.
(Tune: 'Here we go round the mulberry bush')

Say goodnight, say goodnight,
sleep in peace, sleep in peace.
All my love surrounds you,
all my love surrounds you.
God bless you, God bless you.
(Tune: 'Frère Jacques')

He's got the whole world in his hands.
He's got the whole wide world in his hands.
He's got the whole world in his hands. (x2)

He's got [add individual names] in his hands (x3)
He's got the whole world in his hands.
(Traditional tune)

Be near me, Lord Jesus,
I ask thee to stay
close by me for ever
and love me, I pray.
Bless all the dear children
in thy tender care,
and fit us for heaven
to live with thee there.
(Verse 3 of 'Away in a manger')

Being part of the community of faith

Coming to church is an important part of being a member of God's family. It's about:

- **being with God**: getting to know God, expressing our love for God and enjoying his love for us;
- **being with one another**: supporting and learning from one another on our journey of life and faith.

When we come to church, we come into the presence of God. We bring with us in our minds and hearts all that has happened to us in the days and weeks that have just passed – our hopes and dreams, our fears, our regrets, the situations and decisions about which we need guidance, the burdens we carry for ourselves and for others. At the end of a service, we go out with God's blessing to face whatever is in store for us, knowing that God goes with us.

So, of course, God isn't just in church – he's everywhere, and Jesus said that the important thing is to worship God 'in spirit and in truth'. But church is helpful because:

- meeting together means we can support one another in our faith and in our lives;
- the Bible readings, sermon, and words and actions in the service help us come to know God better;
- our encounters with God in church help us to find the strength to live as God's people in the world.

Travelling together

A child's baptism is a great time to think about where you are on your own journey of faith. If you're new to church or if it's been a long time since you were part of a church, or even if you come to church every week but haven't had a chance to ask the big questions you've always wondered about, then you might enjoy meeting up regularly or occasionally with others in a similar situation to 'travel together'. Many churches organize such groups – why not see if your church has a group you could join?

Resources

Bibles
Reading the Bible is important on your journey of faith. But it's a big book and there are lots of different versions. It's best to choose one that you can understand.

Three of the most popular modern translations are:
New Revised Standard Version (many churches use this version)
Contemporary English Version (a more contemporary style)
Good News Bible (a straightforward modern version)

There are some wonderful children's Bibles available for all different age groups. Here are some of the most popular ones:
Baby's Hug-a-Bible, Sally Lloyd-Jones and Claudine Gevry (HarperFestival, 2010)
The Lion First Bible, Pat Alexander (Lion Hudson, 2008)
The Usborne Children's Bible, Heather Amery and Linda Edwards (Usborne Publishing, 2009).

Prayer books
When you find it hard to express your prayers in your own words, prayer books can be helpful. Here are some suggestions:
The SPCK Book of Christian Prayer (SPCK, 2009)
Pocket Prayers: The classic collection, Christopher Herbert (Church House Publishing, 2009)
Pocket Prayers for Children, Christopher Herbert (Church House Publishing, 2009).

Two useful books on the Christian life for adults are:
How to Pray: A practical handbook, John Pritchard (SPCK, 2011)
Do Nothing to Change Your Life, Stephen Cottrell (Church House Publishing, 2007).

There are many well-illustrated books of prayers for children, including:
My Very First Prayers, Lois Rock and Alex Ayliffe (Lion Hudson, 2003)
Baby Prayers, Sarah Toulmin and Kristina Stephenson (Lion Hudson, 2007)
The Lion Book of Prayers for Children, Rebecca Winter and Helen Cann (Lion Publishing, 2009).

Websites
For more about the Christian faith, visit www.rejesus.co.uk

For more on godparents (including the legal requirements):
http://www.churchofengland.org/weddings-baptisms-funerals/baptism-confirmation/baptism/becoming-a-godparent-in-the-church-of-england.aspx

For more about children's spirituality and helping children to grow in faith, visit:
www.spiritualchild.co.uk
www.faithinhomes.org.uk
www.themothersunion.org/flourishing_relationships.aspx
www.faithink.com/Inkubators/faith5.asp

To find out about your local churches, visit www.achurchnearyou.org

To find out about other SPCK books and resources, visit www.spckpublishing.co.uk